The Last Sushi

Cartoons from *Mail & Guardian, Sunday Times* and *The Times*

JACANA

Acknowledgements: Thanks to my editors at the Mail & Guardian *(Nic Dawes), at the* Sunday Times *(Ray Hartley) and at* The Times *(Phylicia Oppelt) and the production staff at all the newspapers; my website, ePublications and rights Manager Richard Hainebach; my assistant Eleanora Bresler; Bridget Impey, Russell Martin and all at Jacana; Claudine Willatt-Bate; Nomalizo Ndlazi; and as always my family: Tevya, Nina and my wife Karina.*

10 Orange Street
Sunnyside
Auckland Park 2092
South Africa
(+27 11) 628-3200
www.jacana.co.za

in association with

2011 Jonathan Shapiro

ISBN 978-1-4314-0253-3

Cover design by Jonathan Shapiro

Page layout by Claudine Willatt-Bate
Printed by Ultra Litho (Pty) Ltd, Johannesburg
Job No. 001610

See a complete list of Jacana titles at www.jacana.co.za

For Marjory, my other mother

Other ZAPIRO books

The Madiba Years (1996)
The Hole Truth (1997)
End of Part One (1998)
Call Mr Delivery (1999)
The Devil Made Me Do It! (2000)
The ANC Went in 4x4 (2001)
Bushwhacked (2002)
Dr Do-Little and the African Potato (2003)
Long Walk to Free Time (2004)
Is There a Spin Doctor In the House? (2005)
Da Zuma Code (2006)
Take Two Veg and Call Me In the Morning (2007)
Pirates of Polokwane (2008)
Don't Mess With the President's Head (2009)
Do You Know Who I Am?! (2010)

7 October 2010

Fifa pressure was behind the positioning of the stadium soon to be the burden of
Cape Town ratepayers after being abandoned by its French operators due to heavy losses

5 October 2010

Without naming Julius Malema, Cosatu general secretary Zwelenzima Vavi calls for political hyenas buying support in the Youth League to be exposed

Eye-popping claim made by the SA Communist Party's general secretary
as he talks up the ANC's proposed media appeals tribunal

10 October 2010

Often shooting from a helicopter, poachers have killed 225 rhinos this year.
Facing charges is a syndicate which includes conservation officials.

7 October 2010

17 October 2010

Senior editors meet with a government delegation to raise concerns over the Protection of Information Bill and proposed media tribunal

21 October 2010

11th-hour resignations of five senior journalists scupper the launch of the newspaper
that's funded by the ANC-linked Gupta family and aims to be supportive of government

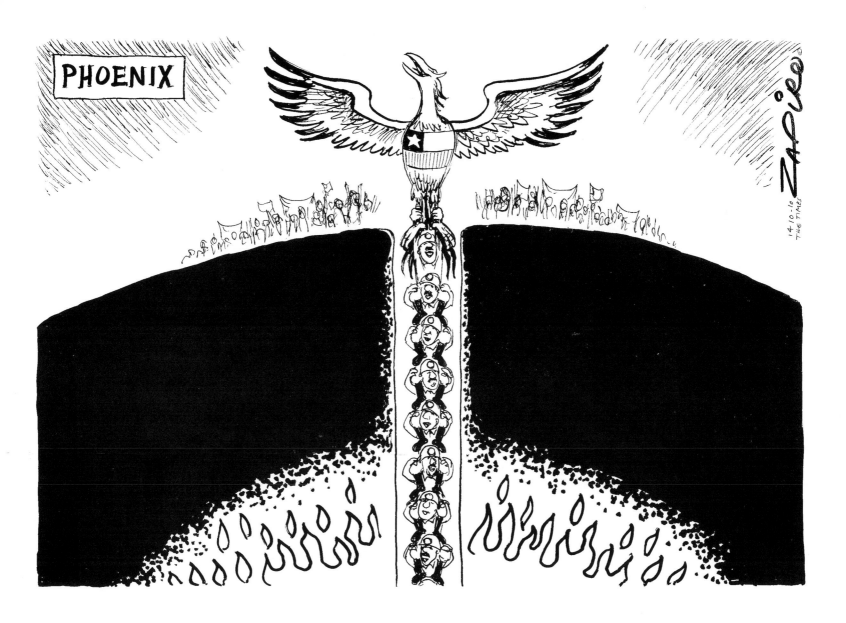

PHOENIX

The 33 Chilean miners trapped deep underground for 69 days are hauled up
one by one in a capsule named Phoenix via a 625m rescue tunnel

14 October 2010

11

THE BIGGEST LOSER

THE KARDASHIANS

BIG BROTHER

THE REAL REALITY TV

19 October 2010

There's a decade of evidence but Hawk's boss Anwar Dramat
finds nothing useful and shuts down the arms deal probe

13

Julius Malema can blow off rumours of illicit perks but his week is a series of unfortunate events

24 October 2010

It's not just *any* minister's wife who's appearing in court, charged with
international cocaine trafficking using young women as drug mules

THE TIMES 26-10-10 ZAPiro

26 October 2010

Consumed by the leadership battle between interim party president Mosiuoa Lekota
and now-suspended deputy Mbhazima Shilowa, Cope is broke and may split

16

28 October 2010   Cold comfort for many as Finance Minister presents his medium-term budget policy statement

28 October 2010

After his scathing 'Dear Government' letter sparks controversy, Idols judge Gareth Cliff
apologises and meets presidential spokesman Zizi Kodwa for a cordial lunch

31 October 2010

Now Vavi calls BEE-types who flaunt their wealth hyenas
and names corruption as the biggest threat to democracy

4 November 2010

IT tycoon Robert Gumede launches a flimsy smear campaign against the *Mail & Guardian*'s investigative team − the Dungbeetles − in response to their tough questions

9 November 2010

'No evidence to proceed' is what they told us when they closed the case. Now British auditing probe names the SA politicos and businessmen who pocketed R1 billion in 'commissions'.

Elephantine Aurora boss drives 19 luxury cars and happens to be the president's nephew.
1200 miners on two mismanaged mines haven't been paid for eight months.

11 November 2010

22

Raunchy tell-all autobiography

14 November 2010

Two schoolboys captured on cellphone apparently raping a drugged
15-year-old schoolgirl are arrested, spotlighting widespread school abuse

18 November 2010

When it turns out the underage sex incident was consensual,
ever-reliable prosecutions boss Menzi Simelane takes charge

21st
CENTURY

Slight Shift on Condom Policy

23 November 2010

Pope Benedict says condoms can sometimes be the
lesser of two evils when used to curb the spread of HIV/Aids

25 November 2010

SA's largest private healthcare group is prosecuted after admitting it made millions
doing illegal transplants of kidneys bought from poverty-stricken third-world donors

25 November 2010

Aiming to create 5 million jobs, Economic Development Minister Ebrahim Patel
unveils his New Growth Path in a sector crowded with competing appointees

The self-confessed hitmen who killed failed mining magnate Brett Kebble say it was assisted suicide but they've named druglord Glenn Agliotti as the mastermind. He walks free after a bungled prosecution.

28 November 2010

ASSISTED SUICIDE

2 December 2010

30 November 2010

The whistleblower website that leaked 77 000 secret US military documents
causes more embarrassment by leaking 250 000 US diplomatic communiqués

31

MOST FEARED WEAPONRY

19TH CENTURY:
Battleship

20TH CENTURY:
Nukes

5-12-10
SUN. TIMES
ZAPIRO

21ST CENTURY:
Geek with computer

Assange

SEND

Wiki Leaks

Website founder Julian Assange, now in hiding

7 December 2010

Surprise World Cup hosts announced after bribery-ridden bidding war. Is Russia being rewarded for slamming Fifa's critics? Have they even heard of football in Qatar?

21 December 2010

Sepp Blatter hands over SA 2010 profits of $80 million — about an eighth of what Fifa made.
While in Jo'burg he quips unfunnily that gays should stay celibate during Qatar 2022.

'UK honeymooners hijacked, wife killed' said the headlines that confirmed our crime image.
Now husband Shrien is arrested in Britain on suspicion of masterminding Anni's murder via a hitman.

9 December 2010

35

12 December 2010

Afrikaner author Annelie Botes declares she doesn't like black people
and Afrikaans schlock singer Steve Hofmeyr has an anti-black Facebook rant

THE·LAST·SUSHI

22 December 2010

Year's end. There's been dodgy dealing, wealth flaunting
and bling king Kenny Kunene's naked sushi parties.

37

16 December 2010

Resuscitation of two-year-old defamation lawsuit. It's that 2008
'Rape of Lady Justice' cartoon again. Court case set to start mid-2012.

26 December 2010

13 January 2011

Have marks been doctored? Pass rate jumps by a whopping 7% in a year disrupted by the World Cup and a teachers' strike.

40

350 people sign online petition aiming to unseat him as patron of
two SA Holocaust centres. 2000 quickly sign a petition supporting him.

SUN. TIMES 16·1·11 ZAPIRO

16 January 2011

Six weeks after UN-approved election results confirmed challenger
Alessane Ouattara as the winner, incumbent Laurent Gbagbo won't step down

THE WORLD'S CERTAINTIES

Death...   Taxes...   ..and an axed useless SABC chief will walk away with millions.

After a 6-month suspension for under-performance,
SABC CEO is 'allowed to resign' with a R3.4 million payout

23 January 2011

Police chief's comment that a 'monkey came from London to have his wife killed here' has been seized upon by lawyers trying to prevent Shrien Dewani's extradition to SA

The uprising against Ben Ali's 23-year dictatorship began just
a month ago and word spread via Twitter and Facebook. He's been
forced to step down and protests have been sparked across the Arab world.

20 January 2011

27 January 2011

Now Egypt erupts as thousands take to the streets, met by
the violent crackdown of President Hosni Mubarak's police

1 February 2011

Mubarak's appointment of a deputy is the first hint of an exit strategy
as protests rage across Egypt in defiance of his crackdown

47

Researchers call for overhaul of registration so that the upcoming election can't be rigged

27 January 2011

Mangosuthu Buthelezi has led the ailing Inkatha Freedom Party for 30 years. When party chairman Zanele Magwaza-Msibi fails to unseat him, she forms the National Freedom Party.

Two weeks ago a Twitter report claimed Madiba had died. Days later,
his minders' cryptic statement that he was hospitalised for 'routine tests'
fuelled panic. Relief all round when he emerges after treatment for pneumonia.

30 January 2011

3 February 2011

Trademark opulence and naked sushi at the launch of Kenny Kunene's latest nightclub,
as well as a speech by his crony Malema claiming the club for the ANC

Failure of Joburg's new billing system sees
40 000 ratepayers cut off for not paying grossly inflated bills

New position for the Black Management Forum head who's best known
for bad relations with the press and for stirring racial controversy

3 February 2011

A N C Heaven

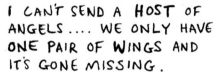

8 February 2011

At a party rally, President Zuma tells the crowd they'll go to heaven
if they vote ANC and to hell if they vote for the opposition

10 February 2011

Ahead of the State of the Nation Address. In last year's speech
he promised a year of action on jobs and delivery.

This year, at least his presentation is somewhat less stilted

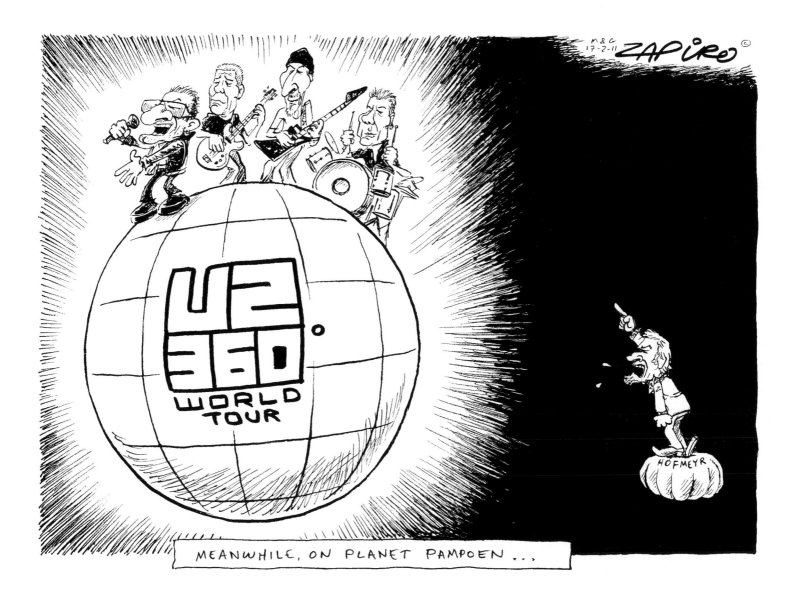

MEANWHILE, ON PLANET PAMPOEN ...

Asked about the 'Shoot the Boer' furore, Bono expressed general support
for struggle songs. Steve Hofmeyr reacts by chucking his U2 tickets into the
Jukskei River and tweeting a 'Shoot the Boer' parody of 'Sunday Bloody Sunday'.

17 February 2011

17 February 2011

Democratic Alliance leader Helen Zille: the party that slams curtailment of media has removed
Sowetan correspondent Anna Majavu from their mailing list because of her 'biased' reports

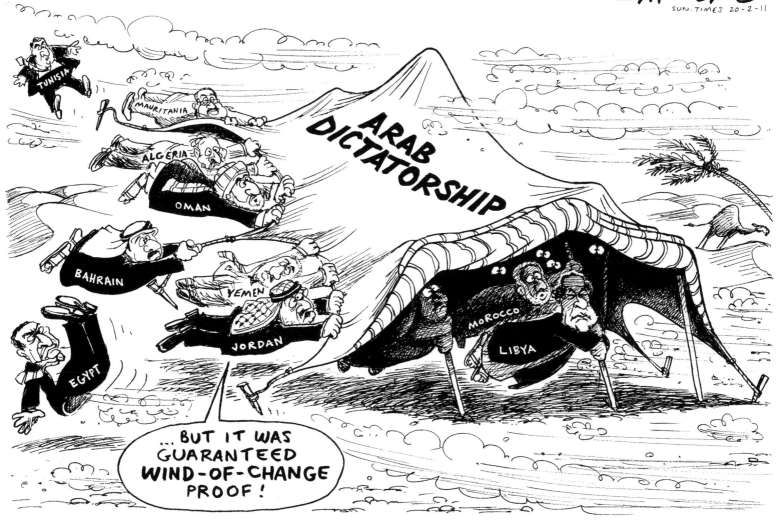

20 February 2011

More protests, more clampdowns, more teetering regimes

Full-fledged uprising in Libya with some areas under rebel control and 600 dead.
Brother Leader makes a characteristically unhinged speech inciting his militiamen to spill blood.

24 February 2011

1 March 2011

Zuma's under party pressure over the Guptas' growing influence
and the megadeals they've secured for his son and nephew

3 March 2011

Before he became government spokesperson, Jimmy Manyi said there was an over-supply of coloureds in the Western Cape. Minister in the Presidency Trevor Manuel calls him a racist in the mould of HF Verwoerd.

Bluster from Cele after Public Protector Thuli Madonsela finds him
and Public Works Minister Susan Shabangu guilty of improper conduct
for authorising a dodgy R500-million lease for the new police HQ in Pretoria

27 February 2011

3 March 2011

Plainclothes cops raid Madonsela's office in search of documents
she used in her probe. Police top brass claim the visit was unauthorised.

6 March 2011   Welcome home. Or maybe not.

66

Though another Manyi racist jibe has come to light — he said Indians bargained their way to the top — it seems it's Manuel who's under pressure for publicly challenging a government colleague

8 March 2011

10 March 2011

Sure enough, he's left isolated. The ANC rebukes him for
acting like a free agent and government expresses confidence in Manyi.

68

Madonsela to meet government over her bombshell report.
And she's demanding answers from police bosses about the raid on her office.

10 March 2011

69

Released on medical parole two years ago due to 'terminal illness',
convicted fraudster Schabir Shaik is re-arrested following reports that
he punched a man at a mosque and assaulted a journalist while playing golf

15 March 2011

@ZAPIRO
SUN. TIMES 13-3-11
After Hokusai's
'The Great Wave'

13 March 2011

Magnitude 8.9 quake unleashes cataclysmic tsunami that devastates
north-eastern Japan. Thousands are killed and thousands more are missing.

17 March 2011

Explosion of quake-crippled Fukushima plant causes radiation leakage,
near-meltdown and alarm about the safety of ageing nuclear facilities worldwide

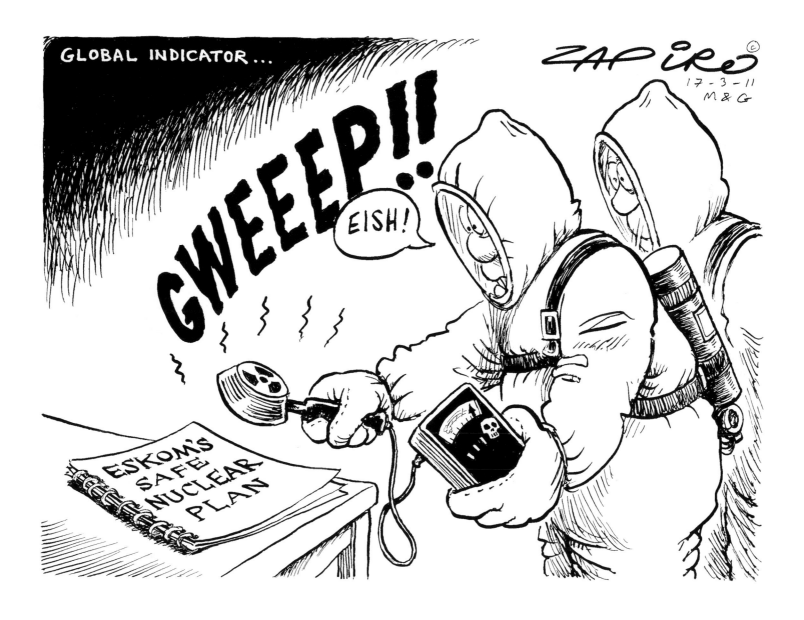

17 March 2011

Nuclear shutdowns on three continents. Nicely timed, our energy supplier
releases its expanded programme which doubles our reliance on nukes.

20 March 2011

As Gaddafi's forces pummel rebel-held civilian areas, the UN Security Council
authorises a no-fly zone − code for air strikes − over Libya. SA votes hesitantly in favour.

24 March 2011

Tightening the screws on an old chum is awkward,
especially when he helped bankroll your rise to power

22 March 2011   'Insufficiently insulated from political interference' is the Constitutional Court's verdict

24 March 2011

Fears of groundwater contamination if oil giant Shell gets the go-ahead
to drill for natural gas using a process called hydraulic fracturing, or fracking

Another World Cup, another mental meltdown.
In Bangladesh we fold in the quarter-finals against lower-ranked New Zealand.

27 March 2011

Seems the Czech mobster who's up for murder has been
running his crime network with the help of top cops. Now jittery
crime intelligence bosses are spying on the Hawks who're probing them.

29 March 2011

Dirty infighting. General Richard Mdluli and three other crime intelligence honchos linked to Krejcir are arrested for a decade-old murder. They happen to be allies of jailed former police commissioner Jackie Selebi, and they've been digging the dirt on current commissioner, General Cele.

3 April 2011

7 April 2011

Five months after elections, bad loser Laurent Gbagbo is holed up beneath the presidential palace. UN-assisted troops loyal to president-elect Ouattara are closing in.

5 April 2011

We voted for Nato air strikes against Gaddafi and then condemned air strikes. And we perversely backed election-reject Gbagbo's inclusion in power-sharing − until events overtook our position.

14 April 2011

Pro-democracy protests spotlight human rights abuses and
royal opulence in the kingdom where political parties are banned

12 April 2011   Activists want Zuma to intervene in Swaziland but SA hasn't taken a formal stance

7 April 2011   Vavi warns that the rot in the ANC could cost the party in the upcoming local government elections

10 April 2011

Stooping low in a speech at a party rally

Sued for hate speech by AfriForum for singing the controversial 'Shoot the Boer'
struggle song, Malema appears in the Equality Court. Meanwhile, outrage erupts over
shocking TV footage of an unarmed protester being beaten and shot to death by six policemen.

14 April 2011

21 April 2011

In Ficksburg, apologising to the bereaved family

Sicelo Shiceka paid for family air trips and five-star hotels and spent
over R1 million to visit his jailed lover in Switzerland – all at taxpayers' expense.
Conveniently for ministers, the handbook outlining their perks is classified.

17 April 2011

19 April 2011

Grumbling ANC secretary-general Gwede Mantashe

At Easter, it's three weeks till we vote

24 April 2011

26 April 2011

'Shoot the Boer' hate speech trial. No verdict yet, but televised
hearings show a composed Malema lecturing his bumbling accusers.

28 April 2011   Kate Middleton to marry William Whatsisname

94

3 May 2011

On a secret Presidential mission, US Navy Seals shoot
Osama bin Laden dead at his clandestine compound in Pakistan.

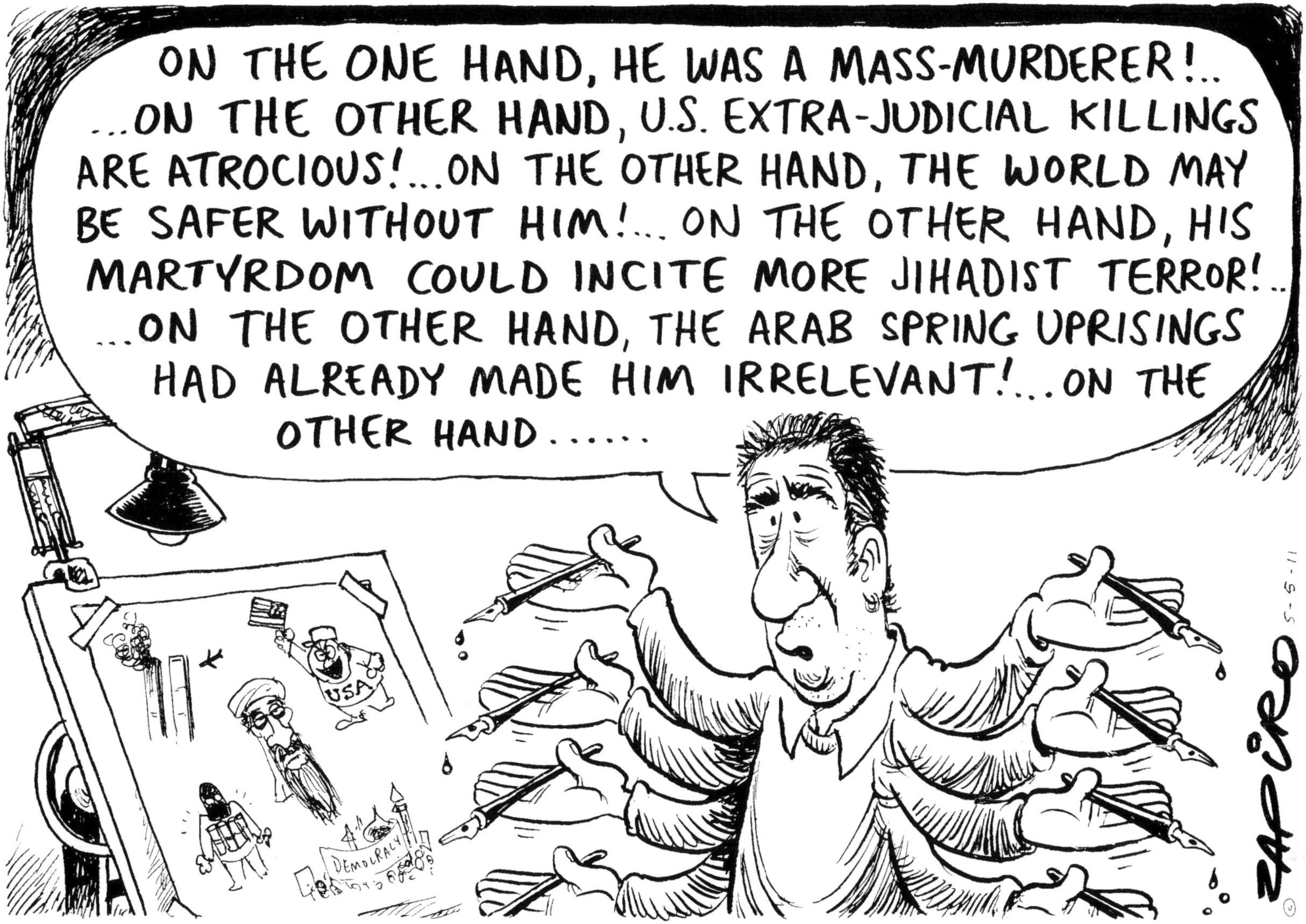
ON THE ONE HAND, HE WAS A MASS-MURDERER!.. ...ON THE OTHER HAND, U.S. EXTRA-JUDICIAL KILLINGS ARE ATROCIOUS!...ON THE OTHER HAND, THE WORLD MAY BE SAFER WITHOUT HIM!... ON THE OTHER HAND, HIS MARTYRDOM COULD INCITE MORE JIHADIST TERROR!.. ...ON THE OTHER HAND, THE ARAB SPRING UPRISINGS HAD ALREADY MADE HIM IRRELEVANT!...ON THE OTHER HAND......
USA
DEMOCRACY
5-5-11

5 May 2011

5 May 2011

8 May 2011

Siyabonga Cwele's wife Sheryl found guilty

After months of kicking up a stink over open toilets in the
Western Cape, the ANC is found to be in a similar mess elsewhere

15 May 2011

The ANC isn't responsible for Moqhaka's open toilets, says Malema while visiting. Yet the party's councillors built them and profiteered from them and the minister knew about this for a year.

Election results. The Democratic Alliance cements its grip
on the Western Cape and grows its national support by 65%.

19 May 2011

17 May 2011

19 May 2011   While the ANC still controls most major cities, its drop in support is seen as punishment for 'jobs for pals'

22 May 2011   US preacher Harold Camping has been proclaiming May 21 (yesterday) as Judgement Day

24 May 2011

Speaking in Washington, Israeli premier Binyamin Netanyahu spurns
President Obama's warning over Israel's intransigence and instead receives
ovations for rejecting a Palestinian state based on Israel's pre-1967 borders

26 May 2011

Little Jack Warner

sat in a corner
eating his FIFA pie

He put in his thumb
and pulled out a plumb

..and said:
"Sepp's as guilty as I!"

31 May 2011

Was Qatar's 2022 World Cup 'bought'? When Fifa heavyweights Jack Warner and
Mohamed bin Hammam hear they're being probed, Warner threatens to implicate Blatter.

9 June 2011

Nato-led alliance intensifies airstrikes on Libya. Meanwhile, Blatter is re-elected unopposed after his sole challenger is taken out by bribery charges.

Fears of retrenchments and of a market flooded with cheap imports
as Massmart's merger with US retail giant, Walmart, is approved

2 June 2011

5 June 2011   Albertina Sisulu, struggle icon and lifelong partner of Walter Sisulu, dies aged 92

29 May 2011

Eastern Cape regional leader Nceba Faku incites his followers
to burn the newspaper that's exposed his involvement in tender fraud

9 June 2011

In parliament, railroading begins of the draconian Protection of Information Bill (dubbed the Secrecy Bill). And they let on that they're pushing ahead with the planned media appeals tribunal.

12 June 2011

The state's chief spokesman is at it again. He chides media reporting,
saying those that 'tell the truth' will be favoured with government advertising.

19 June 2011

7 June 2011

Ahead of the Youth League's elective conference, saying that
'Mbeki is the best leader the ANC has ever produced' is a clear swipe at Zuma

Vavi has warned of what will happen if Youth League populists
succeed in ousting top ANC leaders in 2012. And he's branded Malema's
calls for nationalisation as a scheme to rescue debt-laden BEE mine-owners.

14 June 2011

16 June 2011

Resoundingly re-elected as Youth League president after his tirade against Cosatu
and the Communist Party for criticising nationalisation without offering alternatives

21 June 2011

Fiery victory speech demanding nationalisation (naturally) and land expropriation
without compensation, and declaring 'war' on anyone opposing these policies

Outspoken struggle veteran and former education minister
dies aged 76, having recently slammed the Protection of
Information Bill and the tendency to use politics for personal gain

23 June 2011

Swedish company SAAB outs its UK partner, BAE, for paying
huge 'bonuses' to SA consultant Fana Hlongwane in the Gripen fighter jet deals.
Next, BAE's secret payment channel is outed. Pressure mounts to reopen investigations.

30 June 2011

3 July 2011

Cosatu's four-day review conference opens with the
general secretary's hard-hitting report but it's downhill from there

12 July 2011

Top corruption busters Thuli Madonsela and Willie Hofmeyr suddenly have
corruption claims levelled at them — hers by police, his by the NPA. Smells of a pattern.

14 July 2011

Repeated use of the F-word is the Youth League spokesman's response when a journalist phones him with a tough question. And it's his third such tirade this year.

14 July 2011

After a bloody 56-year fight for independence, Africa's newest nation is born, with Salva Kiir as president. South Sudan gets most of the oil resources and not a lot else.

DINGBATS

(with apologies to DILBERT)

an absurd workplace comic strip

THE BOSSES

WE WON'T GIVE IN TO WORKERS' GREED!

STRIKE
WE DEMAND 13%

MY 28% INCREASE

THE WORKERS

LET'S WIN PUBLIC SYMPATHY BY TRASHING THE CITY!!!

BRILLIANT!

STRIKE

THE UNIONISTS

OUR GOALS FOR JULY:

BRING THE ECONOMY TO ITS KNEES AND GET ANOTHER LOTTO MILLION FOR OUR UNION BASH!

WHAT ABOUT THE UNEMPLOYED?

FORGET IT! ..YOU'RE NOT IN THE PICTURE.

 ZAPIRO THE TIMES 21-7-11

21 July 2011

Annual strike season

17 July 2011   As people give '67 minutes for Mandela' on his birthday, a fuel industry strike has seen pumps run dry

19 July 2011

Growing clamour for the axing of the dodgy cop and the two dodgy ministers

Illegal phone hacking scandal forces media mogul Rupert Murdoch to shut down *News of the World,* fire top execs and shelve his expansion plans

21 July 2011

24 July 2011   Apartheid's general, former Defence Minister Magnus Malan, dies unrepentant at 81

26 July 2011

The death at 27 of Amy Winehouse is unexplained, though she's as
famous for her battles with substance abuse as she is for her singing brilliance

Clamour for Malema's finances to be probed after *City Press* reveals how
he is bankrolled: payments into a secret trust from a construction boss
who won R200 million in tenders in his powerbase province of Limpopo

28 July 2011

28 July 2011   Investigated by three state agencies

ERIC MIYENI

M&G 4·8·11   ZAPIRO ©

Sowetan columnist damns *City Press* for exposing Malema's finances
and labels editor Ferial Haffajee a 'black snake in the grass' who would
'probably have had a burning tyre around her neck' in the 1980s

4 August 2011

135

Every legal expert except the President's has said his extension of Chief Justice Sandile Ngcobo's term needs re-working to be constitutionally valid. Surprise surprise, the respected judge withdraws before the deadline and is lost to the court.

2 August 2011   Recent admissions in Europe prompt Hawks boss Anwar Dramat to contact investigators there

4 August 2011

Forensic audit finds that Cricket SA's CEO Gerald Majola
secretly authorised R4 million in bonuses for himself

7 August 2011

Blockbuster movie released as Congress passes a last-ditch deal
to raise the US borrowing limit and avoid a debt default crisis

UK court rules that the alleged honeymoon murder mastermind should stand trial in South Africa. London is burning as a protest against a police shooting erupts into full-blown riots.

11 August 2011

14 August 2011

Health Minister Dr Aaron Motsoaledi is upbeat when outlining the planned
National Health Insurance scheme. Implementing it in shambolic hospitals will be another story.

Zuma yells at Malema for barging in on a high-level ANC meeting
about whether to discipline Malema for various violations of party policy

16 August 2011

He is told he'll face a hearing soon and be charged for demanding
regime change in Botswana and for other divisive statements

21 August 2011

143

23 August 2011   Tripoli falls to the rebels. Gaddafi has disappeared and is rumoured to be seeking asylum in South Africa.

President Bashar al-Assad's forces have used heavy weaponry to
stem the uprising in Syria. The regime forbids caricatures of the president.

1 September 2011

25 August 2011

Catching flak after asking wealthy whites to pay a reparations tax for benefiting from apartheid. He's also lamented how cadre deployment unfairly enriches a clique.

Nominating Concourt's new head, Zuma again overlooks independent-minded Deputy
Chief Justice Dikgang Moseneke, opting instead for Mogoeng Mogoeng, a former lackey judge
in an apartheid homeland and an evangelical conservative with a record of sexism and homophobia

18 August 2011

28 August 2011

While Mogoeng Mogoeng's flaky judgments fuel public opposition to his nomination,
chances are he'll soon be rubber-stamped by the Judicial Service Commission

4 September 2011

The bill that's a step closer to becoming law excludes any protection for whistleblowers and journalists who reveal state secrets that expose official wrongdoing

6 September 2011

8 September 2011

THE PIMVILLE METHODIST EPISCOPAL CHURCH
HYMNSHEET

Jesus, Tender Shepherd, Hear Me

O Come, Youth League Faithful

Stand Up, Stand Up, for Julius!

How Fake Thou Art

Hark the Herald Angels Sing,
Glory to My New-found Bling

Mine Eyes Have Seen the Glory
of Committing Tender Fraud

All Things Breitling and Beautiful

30 August 2011

1 September 2011

13 September 2011

WHAT CRASS OFFICIAL BLOW IS PORTRAYED HERE?

a. Judge Colin Lamont's ban on singing "Dubhul' iBhunu"

b. The ANC's ramming through of the Info Bill without a public interest clause

c. Both of the above, which is why we're in such trouble.

15 September 2011

15 September 2011

18 September 2011

20 September 2011

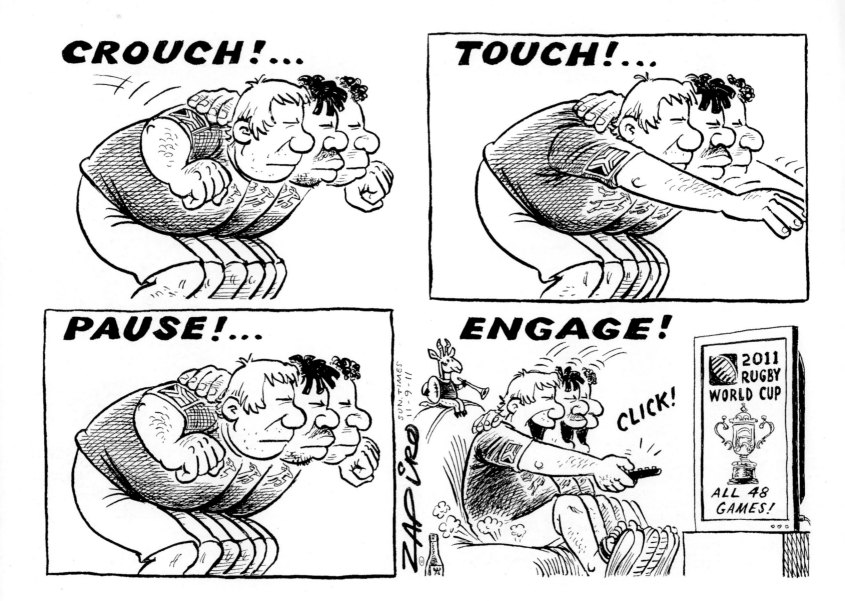

11 September 2011